NATIONAL GEOGRAPHIC

READING EXPEDITIONS®

IMMIGRATION

Erik's Story
From Sweden to Minnesota

By Ann Rossi
Illustrated by Chris Hahner

PICTURE CREDITS
Page borders, 5 (bottom) © Digital Vision/Getty
Images; 4 Mapping Specialists, Ltd.; 5 (top) ©
S. Halling/PanStock/National Geographic Image
Collection; 60, 61 (bottom) Library of Congress; 61
(top) © Christian Lagereek/Getty Images; 62 ©
Minnesota Historical Society/Corbis; 64 (top) ©
Smithsonian American Art Museum/Art Resource,
(bottom) © Patrick Bennett/Getty Images.

**PUBLISHED BY THE NATIONAL
GEOGRAPHIC SOCIETY**
Produced through the worldwide resources of the
National Geographic Society, John M. Fahey, Jr.,
President and Chief Executive Officer;
Gilbert M. Grosvenor, Chairman of the Board.

**PREPARED BY NATIONAL GEOGRAPHIC
SCHOOL PUBLISHING**
Sheron Long, Chief Executive Officer; Samuel
Gesumaria, President; Francis Downey, Vice
President and Publisher; Richard Easby, Editorial
Manager; Anne M. Stone, Editor; Margaret
Sidlosky, Director of Design and Illustrations;
Jim Hiscott, Design Manager; Cynthia Olson,
Ruth AnnThompson, Art Directors; Matt
Wascavage,Director of Publishing Services;
Lisa Pergolizzi, Production Manager.

MANUFACTURING AND QUALITY CONTROL
Christopher A. Liedel, Chief Financial Officer;
Phillip L. Schlosser, Vice President; Clifton M.
Brown III, Director.

CONSULTANT
Mary Anne Wengel

BOOK DESIGN
Artful Doodlers and Insight Design Concepts Ltd.

Published by the National Geographic Society
1145 17th Street N.W.
Washington, D.C. 20036-4688

Product #4U1005082
ISBN: 978-1-4263-5075-7

Printed in Mexico

15 14 13
10 9 8 7 6 5 4 3

CONTENTS

LEAVING HOME

The United States is a nation of immigrants. These are people who have moved to a new place, leaving the country where they were born. Some people have come to escape from wars, conflict, or hunger at home. Others have come to find freedom and new opportunities. Whatever the reason, this country has grown thanks to waves of immigrants. One of these waves came from Sweden in the 1860s.

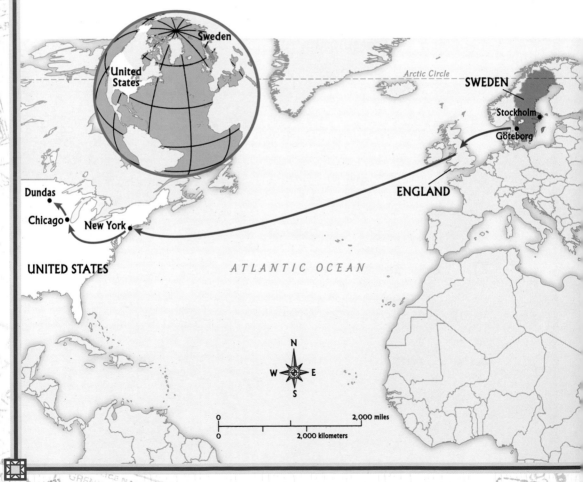

SWEDEN

Geography Sweden is a country in northern Europe. It is about the size of California. Most of the land in Sweden is flat plains or rolling hills. The country is dotted with many lakes, bogs, and marshes. Northern and central Sweden have large spruce and pine forests. Southern Sweden has fertile farmland and miles of coastline.

The People Most Swedes live in the south. In the past, many were farmers or seafarers. Today 85 percent of the people live and work in cities. Important industries include steel, cars, paper products, and telecommunications. Fishing is still a big part of the economy, but only about 2 percent of people still work in farming.

THE EDLUND FAMILY

Amalia Edlund & Baby Freya

Mama Edlund is worried about the future. She wants her children to have land of their own to farm when they grow up.

Oscar

Four-year-old Oscar is fun-loving and sometimes gets into mischief.

Erik

Erik is eleven years old. He lives with his family on a small farm in southern Sweden in 1868. Times are hard. Being the oldest child, Erik wants to do his part to help out.

Sven Edlund
Papa Edlund is a hardworking farmer, but bad weather has ruined his crops. Now the livestock are thin and there is not enough food for his family.

Anders Malmgren
Uncle Anders, Mama's brother, has taken his family to America and settled in Minnesota. He writes letters telling the Edlunds about the success of the Minnesota farm.

Anna
Erik's sister Anna is nine years old. She is a cheerful girl who looks up to her older brother.

CHAPTER 1

A Big Decision

"Erik, *vakna*," said Papa as he gently shook Erik's shoulder. "It's time to get up. We have chores to do."

Eleven-year-old Erik rubbed the sleep from his eyes and tumbled out of bed. His four-year-old brother, Oscar, was still fast asleep. Erik pulled on his clothes in the darkened room. His stomach rumbled as he followed Papa quietly to the door.

These days Erik was always hungry. It seemed the only time his family had enough to eat was on a holiday. Then fish, ham, cheeses, breads, and potatoes crowded the table. Erik's stomach rumbled again at the thought of all that food.

"Come have breakfast after you've seen to the cows," said Mama, looking up from dressing baby Freya.

Erik opened the door and stepped into the dusty farmyard. He trudged to the barn with his dog, Tip.

Even though it was early, the sun had risen. The day was unusually hot for the end of June in Sweden.

Inside the barn, Erik grabbed a pail and began to help Papa milk the cows. As they milked, nine-year-old Anna came into the barn. "There were only three eggs this morning, Papa," she said.

"Well, that's still better than no eggs," answered Papa. "Take them in to Mama. Then ask Oscar to help you pump water for the chickens and cows."

Erik watched his sister leave the barn. He rubbed his hand slowly along the bony flank of a cow. Then he said in a worried voice, "Papa, the cows are getting thin and giving less milk."

"*Ja.* Yes," agreed Papa. "These past two years have been tough on them. Last year there was too much rain, and our grain rotted. This year it's too dry for grass to grow. So the cows still aren't getting enough to eat. Plus, the heat makes the cows unhappy, and an unhappy cow gives less milk."

"What are we going to do?" asked Erik.

"We will do what we have always done. We will farm our land, milk our cows, and hope that next year will be better," said Papa.

He lifted the milk pails and walked toward the house. Erik hesitated briefly. Then he followed Papa slowly to the house.

After a breakfast of porridge, the children took their baskets and followed the dusty path to the meadow by the woods. Mama had sent them to pick moss. After the rains of last summer and now the **drought,** the family had no grain to grind into flour. Without flour, Mama couldn't bake bread—and without bread, the family would have little to eat. So Mama needed the moss. She would grind it up and add it to the last bit of bread flour. Then she would bake using the moss and flour mixture.

----

drought – an extended time of very little rain

Tip, Oscar, and Anna bounded ahead. But Erik lagged behind. He saw how plants drooped all around. The heat had shriveled them. Erik knew the same thing would happen to their crops if they didn't water them each day. And then what would his family eat?

"Maybe I'll find some *smultron,* wild strawberries for us to eat," said Anna.

"If anyone could find them, you could—but I doubt there are any," said Erik. "It's almost too dry for anything to grow this year. Hard to believe that last year was too wet. Remember?"

"It rained so much that the field over there was flooded," said Anna. "The ducks thought it was a pond and paddled around on it!" She laughed at the memory.

Erik only frowned. "Now we'll have to eat moss bread again," he said gloomily.

"But I don't like moss bread," wailed Oscar sadly. "It tastes funny."

"Look!" crowed Anna. She pointed to some tiny red berries near her feet. *"Smultron!* I knew I'd find some."

Clumps of wild strawberry plants were scattered across the meadow leading up to the woods. Oscar bent down and popped a berry into his mouth. Erik's stomach grumbled. The sight of the juicy berry had made him very hungry.

Eagerly, the children crouched down and alternately picked and ate the tiny strawberries. The juices from the ripe berries stained their fingers crimson. The smell of sweet, sun-warmed strawberries filled the air. Soon the children's chins were dripping with juices. Erik sighed with satisfaction.

"I don't want to pick anymore," announced Oscar.

"Okay. You can play with Tip, but stay where we can see you," cautioned Anna. She and Erik began picking strawberries in earnest. At last they had enough so that everyone would have some for dessert that night. Erik stood up and stretched.

"Mama will be pleased," he said, grinning at Anna. "Now, let's go find that moss." He looked around. "Where's Oscar?"

"I don't know," said Anna. She scanned the meadow. "He was supposed to stay where we could see him. Where could he have gotten to?"

"I don't know, but we'd better find him. Oscar! Tip! Where are you?" called Erik.

The two children looked around frantically. It wasn't like Oscar to wander off. What would they do if they couldn't find him? They called again, "Tip! Oscar!"

To their relief, Tip raised his head at the sound of their voices. He bounded toward Erik and Anna.

"Find Oscar," ordered Erik. Tip cocked his head and trotted back to where he'd been lying down. There, fast asleep in the grass, was Oscar.

"Good boy, Tip," said Erik, hugging the dog. "What would we do without you?" The three children gathered up their strawberries and headed off to the forest.

That night, after a dinner of soup and strawberries, Papa pulled a letter from his pocket and announced, "Uncle Anders has sent us a letter from America. He wrote from Goodhue County, Minnesota. It's dated May 30, 1868." Papa read the letter aloud.

Dear Sister, Brother-in-law, Nephews, and Nieces,

How is the farm? Are your crops doing better than last year? It has been months since we have had any news from Sweden.

Life isn't easy here in America, but we are doing well. I'm amazed how good the soil is. Last year the cornfields looked like a forest. We're hoping for another fine harvest this year.

If things are not looking up in Sweden, you should think about coming to America. Land sells quickly, but there are still good plots for sale in Minnesota. We could help you get started on a new farm.

We're having the neighbors over next month for Midsummer's Eve. Alma is already planning what we'll eat—bread, pancakes, and pies. Maybe next year you'll be here to celebrate with us!

Your loving brother and uncle,

Anders

"I want pancakes and pies!" said Oscar.

"Think of meeting Aunt Alma!" added Anna.

"And cornfields that look like forests," marveled Erik. "Can we go to America, Papa?"

"We'll see," said Papa. "You heard what Anders wrote. Life in America isn't easy. Besides, we've got our farm to think of—and our parents. Who will take care of them as they get old? Let's not discuss it any more tonight."

Later though, long after bedtime, Erik awoke and heard his parents talking.

"It's not just our crops," he heard Mama say. "It's also our children's future. The only thing we have to give our children is our land. When we divide it among them, each parcel will be too small to support them. How will they make a living?"

"All these years we've cleared the land and planted, and we've always managed to get by!" said Papa fiercely. "We might have only a little bit of land, but it's ours."

"That's true," said Mama. "But over these past two years we've worn ourselves almost to the bone. No matter how hard we work, we can't make the crops succeed if the weather doesn't cooperate. What will we do if we have another bad harvest next year?"

"Despite what Anders says, things might not be any better if we were to move," said Papa. He drummed his fingers on the table and sighed wearily. "It's a lot of work to clear new land. And besides, moving is expensive. We'd have to start over again."

"It can't be as bad as that," said Mama. "Think of all the Swedes who have overcome those problems!"

"We do know many people with relatives in America," Papa admitted. "Plus, America promises more land than we could ever dream of owning in Sweden. And it would be nice to have a larger farm. Perhaps you're right."

"We could see Anders and his family again!" added Mama. "Do you think we could live close to them?"

For the first time, Mama's voice **faltered** just a bit. "Oh, Sven, do you think we would ever come back? I'd miss our parents, siblings, and friends if we moved. Holidays would be so hard without the familiar faces and traditions."

"If we move to America," Papa said gently, "we might never see our loved ones again. But you're right. We have to think of the children. We've got to take a chance at a better life. Shall we risk it?"

"*Ja,*" Mama agreed. "Let's go to America."

When Erik heard this, his face flushed suddenly with excitement. He lay quietly back in his bed and thought of the changes to come.

- - - - - - - - - - - - - -
falter – to break

CHAPTER 2

The Journey Begins

Two months later, the Edlunds were busy packing their belongings for the trip to America. It would cost too much to take everything with them. So furniture and farm animals would stay behind with Aunt Lena and Uncle Jon. The Edlunds would have to start over once they got to America. But Papa had heard that kitchenware and linens were expensive in America. So the family would take their clothes, blankets, linens, and kitchen things.

Mama packed cheese and hardtack, foods that would not spoil for many weeks. The children were allowed to bring one special belonging. Freya, being a baby, had only her blanket. But Anna and Oscar each chose their favorite stuffed toy. Erik brought the one book he owned. Finally, the trunks were packed.

During their last week at home, relatives and friends stopped by to bid the Edlunds farewell. Excited as Erik had been at first about the move, he had never thought how hard it would be to leave. Now sadness overwhelmed him. The worst was saying goodbye to his grandparents. Grandma and Grandpa hugged everyone tight. Then Grandma Edlund cupped Erik's face in her hands. She whispered sadly, "Let me look at your face one last time so I'll always remember you!"

With a wrench, Erik suddenly realized that he might never see her again. He struggled not to cry as he hugged his grandmother goodbye. Why, oh why, had he ever wanted to leave?

Early the next morning, Uncle Jon and Aunt Lena came to the house. As they helped Papa load the trunks onto the wagon, Erik took one last look inside. He traced his finger along the smooth, worn surface of the pine table that stood in the kitchen. He'd learned to read and write at this table. Now he'd never see it again. Then he went outside and climbed into the wagon.

"We're off," said Uncle Jon, flicking the reins. He would drive them to the train station.

"*Vänta!* Wait!" cried Erik. "We've forgotten Tip!"

"Tip can't come with us," reminded Papa.

"But he's part of our family!" exclaimed Anna.

Erik sprang down from the wagon and buried his face into Tip's silky fur. He began to sob. Aunt Lena gently led him back to the wagon. "We'll take good care of Tip for you," she promised.

The wagon rolled down the road. Anna and Erik turned and watched their childhood home, until the house disappeared from view. "I'll never forget it, will you?" Anna whispered to Erik. "Never!" he said. He wouldn't forget their farm or the sight of Tip sitting patiently, waiting for them to come back home.

By late morning the Edlunds arrived at the crowded train station. Erik caught sight of the train first. He thought it looked vaguely like a monster. It was hulking, black, and noisy. The Edlunds joined the throng of passengers trying to board. They jostled their way through the train to their seats.

The children pressed their faces to the window and searched for Aunt Lena and Uncle Jon on the platform. They waved frantically through the glass as the train pulled away from the station. No one could stay sad for long, though. The excitement of their first train ride soon cheered them up.

Erik listened eagerly to snatches of conversation from other passengers. He learned that most of them were **emigrating** from Sweden to America. Some were families like the Edlunds. But many young people were traveling alone, heading to America to find jobs in the cities or on farms. All were hoping for a better life than they could make in Sweden.

Soon the rhythmic motion of the train lulled Erik to sleep. As he slept, the train sped on. Several hours later he awoke with a start. The train had whistled to a halt

---

emigrate – to leave one country to live in another

in Göteborg, where the Edlunds would begin the next leg of their journey.

Quickly they scrambled off the train. Papa went to find someone with a cart to take their trunks to the ship. The rest of the family huddled together and waited for him to return. Travelers surged around them. Oscar and Anna shrank closer to Mama. Erik kept his eyes on their baggage, to keep any thieves away.

At last Papa returned and the family set off on foot through Göteborg. Horse-drawn carts laden with baggage rumbled over the cobblestone streets.

"Look at all the buildings and shops!" exclaimed Mama as they walked.

"All I see are legs!" wailed Oscar. Papa lifted him onto his shoulders for a better view.

All were amazed at the city sights. Anna stopped to stare at bakery displays of breads and cakes that cost more than the Edlunds could afford. Erik gaped at the bookstores, with their shelves piled high. Mama looked at the fashionably dressed women in clothes so different from her own. And so it continued until the family reached the port. There they joined hordes of people streaming toward a steamship.

"Is that the ship to America?" asked Oscar.

"No, we'll take it across the North Sea to England," explained Erik. "Then we catch a train from one coast of

England to the other. Finally, we sail from England to America." Erik was quite proud he knew this. He and Anna had looked at maps to plot their journey.

Once their trunks arrived, the family boarded the ship. They found a place on the deck and stood looking at the city. As the ship glided slowly away from port, Erik thought about all they had left behind. Were Aunt Lena and Uncle Jon finished with the day's milking? Would they remember to hug Tip and tell him what a good dog he was? The rocky coast grew smaller by the moment. Soon Sweden slipped from view. Erik blinked back tears. Would he ever see his home again?

CHAPTER 3

Crossing the Atlantic

More than a week later, Erik stood on the deck of a different ship. This steamboat was crossing the Atlantic Ocean, bound for America. It had left the city of Liverpool, England, three days before.

Erik shuddered when he remembered his first journey by boat across the North Sea to England. More than once, the slippery deck had sent him sliding over to the rail—and nearly overboard—as the boat tilted and pitched on high waves. How seasick Erik had been! He had thought they would never reach England. It was two days of utter agony.

But so far, this new boat moved gently through the water, and Erik hadn't once been sick. Erik liked being up on deck, even though he was already tired of the endless ocean views. At least here he could breathe fresh air. Sometimes he saw seabirds or schools of fish too.

At night, his family and hundreds of other emigrants slept in a huge, windowless room lined with bunk beds far below deck. Down there, Erik felt cooped up like a chicken in a henhouse. It was crowded and there was no privacy. Even though people tried to move quietly, babies cried during the night. Sometimes people whimpered as they dreamed.

The best thing was talking to the other Swedish passengers, singing, or listening as people played their violins and accordions. When he heard the familiar music, Erik almost felt like he was still in Sweden. Somehow it made the journey easier.

Erik's thoughts were interrupted as the rest of his family joined him at the rail. His father asked in halting English, "Where are you going?"

"I am going to Minnesota," replied Erik, also in English.

Since boarding the boat in Liverpool, the family had spent part of each day learning English from a book Papa had brought. It had lots of useful phrases. Now Erik and his family could introduce themselves and say where they were going. They could even ask simple questions. Yet Erik didn't see the point, since no one could understand the answers. Who would have thought that speaking and listening could be so hard?

Suddenly, Oscar pointed to two gray shapes spouting fountains of water. "Sea monsters!" he said. But they were

only whales. The family watched them until they
disappeared from view.

On the twelfth day of their voyage, Erik pointed to
a distant tree-lined shore. "Is that America?" he asked
eagerly. The family craned to catch their first glimpse
of their new land. "It must be!" exclaimed Papa.

"We're almost there!" said Mama with relief. The
journey had been hardest on her, with Oscar and baby Freya
to care for. It would be good to set foot on land again.

As the ship approached New York, the passengers
crowded onto the deck. Boats big and small filled the
harbor, and buildings loomed on the horizon. The ship
made its way slowly toward land before grinding to a stop
in the harbor.

"What's happening?" asked Erik.

"We have to wait here until health inspectors from
New York examine the passengers and crew," someone
explained. "The authorities don't want diseases such as

smallpox and cholera to spread. If you're healthy, you shouldn't have anything to worry about. But no one who is sick may enter the city."

"What will they do if someone's sick?" asked Anna.

"They'll take the person to a hospital until he is well," came the reply.

That night Erik lay awake worrying. What would happen if health inspectors sent him to a hospital? Would his family go to Minnesota without him? How would he find them again? When he finally fell asleep, he dreamed of wandering unfamiliar streets in search of his family.

In the morning Mama fussed over the children. She did her best to make everyone look neat in their crumpled clothes. She scrubbed their faces and ears with a wet cloth—hard!—but Erik didn't complain. On no account did he want to be separated from his family.

Soon the passengers and their baggage were loaded onto a series of barges. The barges took them from the steamship to Castle Garden, at the tip of the city. There the long process of checking in began.

The hours passed slowly. At last the health inspectors came to examine the Edlunds. One doctor looked into Erik's throat and ears and listened for any sign of a cough. Erik couldn't understand him when he talked. However, the man spoke in a friendly voice and he smiled a lot. Erik smiled back gratefully. Soon the examination was finished.

To their relief, the family was all healthy. "What's going to happen now, Papa?" asked Erik.

"We have to register with the officials. They'll ask us our names, our nationality, and where we are going."

The Edlunds filed into the main hall of Castle Garden, a huge circular room lined with benches and filled with thousands of immigrants. Erik recognized some of them from the boat, but there were many new faces as well. The sounds of different languages filled the crowded hall.

It was all so new and strange! Erik wondered what would happen if Papa didn't understand the official's questions. Would they all get sent back to Sweden?

At long last it was the Edlunds' turn. Papa answered the official's first two questions easily enough—but when the official asked a third question, Papa did not understand. Erik's heart stuck in his throat. He watched as the official called to someone, and another man joined them. The newcomer introduced himself in Swedish. He was an **interpreter!** Now Papa could answer the questions.

The interpreter showed them where they could exchange foreign money into American dollars. He also showed them where a railway agent would sell them train tickets. Best of all, he pointed them toward the washrooms. After three weeks on the move, the family could at last scrub themselves clean.

Once everyone had bathed, Mama opened a trunk and took out clean clothes for the rest of the journey. Then, tempted by the smell of food, they bought some rolls from a bread stand and sat down for a meal. The children bit hungrily into the warm, fresh bread.

Papa went to buy train tickets. Like most immigrants heading west, the Edlunds were eager to be on their way. Already their journey had been long.

---

interpreter – someone who translates between two or more languages

"How much longer before we get to the farm?" asked Erik when the family was safely aboard the train.

"It takes four or five days to reach Chicago," answered Papa. "From Chicago, it's probably another two or three days to Dundas, where Uncle Anders will meet us."

As soon as the train began to move, the children peered out the window at New York City. They passed building after building, many four or five stories tall. The streets were filled with horses pulling all kinds of wagons. There were even horses pulling a trolley that rolled along a track! Men were building what looked like an elevated railway line.

"I thought Göteborg was busy, but New York is even busier!" exclaimed Erik. Oscar and Anna said nothing. They pressed their noses against the glass and watched the city pass by.

As the children looked out the window, New York quickly receded from view. Soon towns, farms, and woods replaced the city. After several hours, darkness fell and the family drifted to sleep.

The days on the train soon blended together. Each day the family looked out the window, practiced English, and stretched their legs at rest stops. They ate and told stories. Erik felt comforted by the sight of woodlands and farms. He still missed Sweden and probably always would. Yet parts of America somehow reminded him of home.

One day, Erik was amazed to see grasslands stretching all the way to the horizon. There were no trees or farms anywhere in sight. It reminded him of the ocean—but this was an ocean of grass.

America was such a big country! By the time they reached Chicago, the Edlunds felt overwhelmed by all they'd seen. They were tired after a week sleeping upright in their seats. But there was at least something familiar in the bustling city of Chicago. Swedish! Lots of people spoke Swedish. The whole family perked up at the sounds of home. They hadn't realized how tiring it was to be surrounded by a new language.

Papa sent Uncle Anders a telegraph from the train station in Chicago. "Now Anders will know when we are arriving," he said.

"Just a few more days and we'll see him," said Mama. Her face brightened at the thought.

Time sped quickly after that. The train still had to cross the Mississippi River, the widest river the Edlunds had ever seen. Then at Minneapolis the family had to rush to change trains one last time. But finally the exhausted, dusty, crumpled travelers arrived in the town of Dundas.

Immediately a voice cried out, "Amalia! Sven! Children!" Uncle Anders embraced them all in a bear hug.

"Oh, Anders!" cried Mama. She noticed the tall, broad-shouldered youth behind him. "Ernst, is that you?

You were just a little boy when I saw you last. You're taller than your father now!"

Ernst loaded the Edlund's trunks into a sturdy, wooden buckboard wagon. Erik helped Oscar and Anna up, then clambered aboard himself. He surveyed the sparse town and the wide, open spaces that surrounded it.

After so many days on the move, he didn't know quite what to feel. He was excited to meet new relatives, yet awed by the size of America. Most of all, he was anxious for the journey to end.

By late afternoon, the wagon arrived at the Malmgren farm. Aunt Alma threw open the door to their white clapboard farmhouse and ran to greet everyone.

"*Välkommen!*" she said. "Welcome!" Cousin Edwin heard the ruckus and came running from the barn to see his cousins. The families were together again.

After washing up, the Edlunds ate their first home-cooked meal in nearly a month. It was all that Erik, Oscar, and Anna had dreamed of. They ate until they could eat no more.

The adults stayed at the table long into the night, laughing and sharing stories. Oscar and Anna soon nodded off. When Erik's eyes began to droop, Aunt Alma showed him to his bed. Snug in the clean sheets, with the sounds of family in his ears, he wondered what tomorrow would bring.

CHAPTER 4

Pitching In

The next morning, Erik was the last to rise. He bounded out of bed and joined everyone at the breakfast table. It felt good to be sitting at a table with his family again. They'd been on the move for nearly a month. Erik tried not to stare at all the food: golden pancakes, slabs of ham, bowls of applesauce, and baskets of bread. Oscar and Anna had mounded their plates high.

"You must be hungry after all that traveling," smiled Aunt Alma. "Eat as much as you like." For the second time in two days, Erik ate until he felt full. As he ate, the adults drank *kaffe*—coffee—and talked about old times.

When everyone was done, the Malmgrens showed their relatives around the farm. It was clear that they had worked hard. In addition to the house, there was a large barn, a horse paddock, and fenced-in fields. Beyond the fields were unplowed meadows, and beyond the meadows were woods and a lake. All of it belonged to Uncle Anders and his family.

"We could never have anything this size in Sweden," said Papa. "There isn't enough land for a farmer to buy."

Uncle Anders told how they'd had the farm for seven years now, each year doing something to improve it. They'd built a small cabin first. Then they'd dug a well, so that Aunt Alma no longer had to haul water from a nearby stream. In time, they'd built a larger house, barn, and woodshed. Papa looked longingly at the well-kept buildings, the farm equipment, and the animals.

"Why is the barn so close to the house?" Erik asked.

"It's handy during our fierce winters," said Aunt
Alma. "We have to care for the animals every day, even in
bad weather. You'll see what I mean soon enough."

Erik looked around him. This part of America looked
almost like Sweden. The woods, lake, stream, and fields
reminded him of home. He patted his full stomach and
thought, "I'm going to like it here."

Later that morning, Papa, Uncle Anders, Ernst, Edwin,
and Erik went to split rails for fences. After the long
journey, the work felt good. Erik enjoyed stretching his
muscles again. Mama and the children stayed behind.
Mama had many questions for Aunt Alma.

"Did it take long to learn English?" she asked first.

"We've picked it up mostly by meeting people," said Aunt Alma. "Anders worked as a farmhand during the harvest and at lumber camps in winter because we needed money to buy supplies. That's where he learned English. In winter, the boys went to school and picked up some English there. I learned from them—and our neighbors."

"Were you ever lonely?" asked Mama.

"Sometimes, but I couldn't think about it. There was always so much to do! When we bought a few more cows, we had too much cream. So I made extra butter. One day a neighbor stopped by to ask if we needed anything from town. He had some milk to sell there. I asked him if he'd mind trying to sell my butter too. Sure enough, it sold! Then I started selling eggs. Now, every couple of weeks, he collects my butter and eggs to sell in town. We don't make much, but it's something."

"Is it expensive to live here?" Mama jiggled baby Freya on her knee.

"It's always expensive when you don't have money! At one point we had to save up for an entire year before we could even afford to send a letter home. But when we didn't have money and needed food, we would **barter** our labor or anything extra we had for something to eat. Luckily, there are plenty of fish, ducks, and other game here. We've learned to take care of ourselves and to appreciate what we have."

The women passed the day catching up on news and doing chores. The men were busy making plans too. During dinner that night, Uncle Anders shared the idea he and Papa had for the winter. They were going north to work at the lumber camps. They would get work chopping down trees or sawing trees into logs.

"But Papa! We've only just arrived," said Erik. "Why do you have to go?"

"We used most of our savings to get here. We need to make some money to buy a farm of our own. Uncle Anders says that the lumber camps pay well, since wood is in high demand. People need it for railroad ties, lumber, and other goods. But don't worry. The work won't start until winter, so we won't leave for another month."

Uncle Anders turned to Erik and said, "Ernst and Edwin are coming with us. We need you to pitch in while

----

barter – to exchange one good or service for another

we're away. I hear you're good at caring for farm animals and doing chores. Do you think you could take charge of the farm this winter?"

"Oh, yes!" said Erik quickly. After all, he'd been milking, chopping wood, feeding the animals, and hauling water for years. Plus, Anna and Oscar could help him, just like at home.

The next month passed quickly. In mid-November it was time for the men to leave. The night before they left, each packed a bundle of thick socks, gloves, and other clothes. These would help keep them warm while they worked in the pine forests of northern Minnesota.

"We'll be cutting wood until the spring thaw, probably in April. If we can, we'll send a letter," said Uncle Anders.

"Won't you be home for Christmas?" asked Anna.

"No, the camp is too far away," said Papa. "But we'll celebrate when we return." The children didn't want to think how many months that would be.

The house seemed empty once the men had left, but there was lots of work to do. Erik spent hours each day caring for the animals and chopping wood. Anna and Oscar hauled water, helped with the animals, and watched baby Freya. Mama and Aunt Alma canned soups and applesauce, and everyone helped do laundry.

One gray winter day, Aunt Alma announced, "It looks and feels like snow. Erik, would you chop some extra wood for the fireplace and stove? Pile it next to the front door. Anna, you'd better bring in some extra buckets of water. You may as well fill the water barrel in the barn too. If it snows too much, we won't be able to get to the pump. I don't want you children to go far from the house today. You'll need to put the animals in the barn when you see the first flakes of snow."

As noon approached, the sky grew grayer and the air colder. The first snowflakes fell while the children were working outdoors.

"It's time to go in, Oscar," said Anna.

"Aw, can't I stay outside and play?" begged Oscar. "I love snow."

"No, you need to go in now. Anna and I have to take care of the animals," said Erik.

Oscar clomped indoors while Erik and Anna led the animals into their stalls and pens. Erik piled extra hay into the stalls, and Anna gave the chickens an extra measure of grain to be sure they would have enough food. By the time they were done, snow was falling quickly.

"This is fun," said Anna. "The falling snow makes everything look fuzzy."

When they went in, Aunt Alma handed Erik a rope and said, "Tie one end of this rope to the outside of the house door and the other to the barn door. Make sure the knots are good and tight. If this is a blizzard, the snow will be so heavy we won't be able to see more than an inch or two in front of us. We'll need to feel our way along the rope to go between the house and the barn so we can care for the animals."

As Erik tied the rope he thought, "This is silly! The barn isn't that far away. Surely we'll be able to find our way there and back in a snowstorm?"

By late afternoon, snow swirled angrily against the windowpanes, and wind shrieked down the chimney. Erik watched the snow mound up on the window ledges, glad to be safe at Aunt Alma's.

"Maybe I should take care of the animals tonight," said Aunt Alma.

"But that's my job, Auntie!" protested Erik.

"Erik and Anna can go together to care for the animals," said Mama as she rocked the baby. "They'll be done more quickly than if Erik goes alone."

The two children bundled up. Even so, Erik gasped when he opened the door and the cold wind hit his face. He grabbed the rope with both hands, and Anna followed him into the blizzard.

"Don't let go of the rope!" yelled Erik to Anna as they fought their way through the deep snow. They struggled to open the barn door and slip inside. The barn smelled of warm animals and sweet hay. Erik fumbled for the matches, struck one, and lit the lantern. The children

removed their hats and scarves and worked swiftly to care for the animals.

When they were done, the children bundled up again. Erik said, "Wait by the door while I put out the light. When I'm next to you, we'll open the door and find the rope. Stick close to me—and whatever you do, don't let go of the rope!"

Blowing snow lashed the children's faces as they leaned into the wind. Slowly they stumbled toward the house, holding fast to the rope with their mittened hands. Suddenly the rope went slack.

"What's happened?" yelled Anna, but her words were blown into the emptiness behind her.

Erik kept moving forward, holding the limp rope in his hands. "I've reached the end of the rope," yelled Erik, "but the house isn't here!" He stretched out one hand, then the other, to feel for the house. "It's got to be here somewhere!"

"No! Don't let go of the rope!" yelled Anna. She grabbed for Erik with one hand. "Come back!"

"They should have finished by now," fretted Mama. "What could be keeping them? I'm going out to the barn to see if anything's wrong."

Mama wrapped her coat tightly around her, opened the door, and felt for the rope. It wasn't there.

"The rope! It's broken!" Mama whirled about frantically. "Quick, I need another rope and a lantern! I have to find the children!"

"There is no other rope!" cried Aunt Alma. "Amalia, you mustn't go out into the blizzard. You'll get lost, and then what would become of Oscar and Freya?"

"But Erik and Anna are out there somewhere!" sobbed Mama.

"We have to wait until the storm's over. Then we'll search for them together," said Aunt Alma.

The night passed slowly. Aunt Alma and Mama stayed up, dozing fitfully. "I should never have agreed to let the children go out in a blizzard," thought Alma. "I knew how dangerous it could be!"

By morning, the storm had petered out. Mama and Aunt Alma readied themselves to search. Suddenly, the door flew open and two snow-encrusted figures tumbled through the door.

"Anna! Erik!" cried Mama with relief. "What happened? Are you all right?"

"We were on our way back from the barn last night when the rope broke," began Erik. "I thought we must be near the house, so I reached out my hands to feel for it. Luckily, Anna grabbed my coat and pulled me back."

Anna continued, "Then we turned around and followed the rope back to the barn. My fingers were so cold I could hardly feel the rope."

"When we got back to the barn," said Erik, "we shook the snow off our clothes. There was plenty of milk, so we didn't go hungry. Then we made beds in the hay and covered ourselves with saddle blankets. I don't think a barn has ever felt so snug. And I'm really glad we had that rope to follow, Aunt Alma. It saved our lives!"

CHAPTER 5

Waiting for News

The months passed quickly. There was always something to do on the farm. Still, people were lonely without Uncle Anders and the others. Every morning Oscar asked eagerly, "Is Papa coming home today?" And every morning Mama answered cautiously, "We'll see."

Then one day in early April, the four men returned. They walked up the path as though they'd only just gone out for a stroll. Oscar whooped with joy. He raced out to greet them. Soon everyone was talking about their winter adventures.

As Papa described the pine forests, Erik felt he was there, staring up at trees that were taller than twenty men standing on one another's shoulders. Papa told how he swung his axe to fell the huge pines, while Uncle Anders and Ernst sawed the trees into logs. Erik felt the thick calluses that covered Papa's palms.

Cousin Edwin described how oxen hauled log-filled sleds over the ice and down to the river. "My job was driving the sleds. I walked next to the oxen and drove them down the path to the river," said Edwin.

"Then what happened to the timber?" asked Erik.

Uncle Anders explained how the river ice broke up when the thaw came. Then workers floated the logs downriver to market.

"Sometimes the logs jammed together, and workers had to push the timbers away from each other. We heard stories about men being crushed between the massive timbers," said Ernst.

Uncle Anders looked around the farm. He said, "I can see you have all done a fine job taking care of the farm. It looks better than ever."

"It does indeed," said Papa. "But it also reminds me that I need to start looking for some land of our own."

"You've only just come back!" cried Erik.

"Surely you can wait a couple of weeks, can't you?" pleaded Mama.

"Don't worry. I'm not going anywhere just yet. We have to start planting, and I need to spend time with all of you. But in a few weeks, I'm heading out again. I've heard that the railroad companies own a lot of land. They'll sell it cheap to anyone who helps lay tracks."

"Will you be closer to us, at least?" asked Mama.

"I'm afraid not. I'll be about 100 miles northwest of here in a place called Kandiyohi County. I'm hoping to buy some land for us there by the end of summer. In any event, I'll be back in time to help with the harvest."

"Don't worry, Amalia," said Uncle Anders. "The rest of you Edlunds should stay here until he returns. You're a big help on the farm—especially baby Freya." He chuckled.

Over the next two weeks, the families settled into new routines. Erik was old enough to help with the planting. He couldn't yet handle a plow, but he helped sow the seeds. Anna took over caring for the animals. She milked the cows and mucked out the barn. Even Oscar had new responsibilities. Papa asked him to look after the chickens.

"You'll need to clean out the chicken coop, gather the eggs, and feed and water the hens every day. It's a big responsibility. Can you handle it?" Papa asked.

Oscar nodded solemnly and asked, "Can I still take the cows out to pasture after they're milked?"

"Of course, and you can bring them back to the barn to be milked in the afternoon," laughed Papa. He knew that most of the cows headed back on their own when they were ready to be milked.

All too soon Papa was ready to leave for Kandiyohi County. Erik hugged his father, hoping that he would find the perfect place for them to live. Then Papa rode away.

Work continued on the farm. Uncle Anders and his sons plowed in April and May. Erik helped sow shortly after each field was plowed. As he worked, Erik imagined he was planting seeds on his family's own farm. Surely next year he would be?

Once the crops were planted, Uncle Anders gathered the children. "Now's a dangerous time for the crops," he said. "I need some brave volunteers to spend time in the fields. Are you brave, Oscar?"

"Yes," whispered Oscar shakily.

"Good," said Uncle Anders. "Greedy birds will try to eat our sprouting crops and the seed corn we've planted. I'll need you, Anna, and Erik to chase the birds away so our crops can grow. That means you'll have to do a lot of running, yelling, and waving your arms about. Can you do that for me?"

"Yes!" shouted Oscar boldly. For the next several weeks, the children shouted and chased after the crows. During the summer, they also removed pests and weeds from the growing crops. The crops flourished in the summer sunshine and with the children's care.

As August approached, Mama anxiously awaited Papa's return. He had been gone almost four months now. There had been no word from him. What if he'd had an accident? Mama drove the worries from her mind. She tried instead to picture the land that Papa had surely bought. "By this time next year," thought Mama, "we will be ready to harvest our own crops!"

Two weeks later, Papa came riding up the path. Mama let out a shout of joy and raced out to meet him. As soon as he had dismounted, she asked, "Did you buy some land?"

Papa drawled slowly, "Well . . . as a matter of fact . . . I did!" He lifted Mama off her feet and twirled her around. The children bombarded Papa with questions. "What is it like?" "Do we have a lake?" "Have you built a house?" Their words tumbled over one another.

Papa laughed and said, "I bought us 160 acres of land. It has a nice patch of trees and some of the richest soil I've seen. It's on a lake. But best of all, our closest neighbors are Swedes like us. Their name is Larson."

Papa explained that the Larsons had been on their land for three years, and their farm was doing very well. After he had bought land, he had gone to the Larsons and offered to help them clear and fence a new field. Then Mr. Larson had loaned Papa his plow so that Papa could clear a bit of his own land.

"The only thing I haven't done is build us a house," said Papa. "I've chopped down a whole lot of trees, though. The wood should be dry enough and ready for building by the time we get there."

Papa continued, "I think we should stay here to help with the harvest. Then we can pack up our belongings and move to our farm. With luck, we'll be able to build a log cabin before the first snowfall. It would just be a temporary home, but at least we'll be on our land."

Erik smiled. He didn't mind pitching in with the work at Uncle Anders and Aunt Alma's place. Yet it would be even better to work their own family land.

A week later, Mama began to pack their trunks.

"I'll be sad to see you go," said Aunt Alma. "It has been wonderful having you to talk to. It makes doing the chores so much more pleasant."

"We'll write often," promised Mama, "and maybe we'll be able to visit once a year too."

"We can help you plant next spring," added Alma. "I know I'll miss you all!"

When the harvest was completed, Papa bought a wagon and team of horses. Then the Edlunds loaded their belongings into the wagon, along with some furniture from Uncle Anders and Aunt Alma. They climbed aboard and began the final leg of their journey.

CHAPTER 6

Home at Last

The Edlunds drove all day every day for a week. They stopped occasionally to rest the horses and to eat. But otherwise they pressed on across the miles. Each day as night approached, they looked for a family who might let them sleep in the barn. Sometimes they had to build a small fire and sleep outdoors, wrapped in blankets.

Finally one afternoon Papa said, "We're almost at the Larsons' place. They made me promise that we'd stay with them while we build our house. Why don't we stop and say hello? Then I'll show you our land."

Mama welcomed the chance to meet their new neighbors. For his part, Erik wished they would go straight on to their land. He missed the farm and his relatives back in Sweden. He wanted to see his new home. Even if there was no house yet. Even if it was only just a patch of land.

The Larsons were chopping and stacking wood when the Edlunds drove up to the barn. Their log cabin was large and tidy. Split-rail fences surrounded their fields.

"*Välkommen!* We've been expecting you!" the Larsons greeted them. "It's good to have new neighbors!"

Mama admired their property. "It's been three years of good, hard work," said Mrs. Larson, looking down at her callused hands. "Every year we clear more land and plant more crops. We've added to our herd. Now we're even selling some of our animals to our neighbors."

"I know you'll want to get started building soon," said Mr. Larson, as he showed the children the cow Papa had bought. "I've already organized a group of neighbors to help you put up a log cabin and a barn. It will only take a couple of days if we work together. Tomorrow I'll ride over and tell them you've arrived."

"*Tack!* Thank you!" said Mama and Papa.

"That's what neighbors are for," said Mr. Larson. "We moved to the area with three other families. We've helped one another build homes and clear land. We've shared our plows, tools, and labor."

Mrs. Larson chimed in, "Each winter, one of the men stays home to help with all our farms while the others go off to the lumber camps. When they return, we share in buying seeds, farm equipment, and provisions. Last year we bought a new plow and all took turns using it."

The Edlunds nodded, glad to be part of a community once more.

"I'll help you unload the wagon," offered Mr. Larson. "You can store your belongings in a corner of the barn. We have stalls for your horses and plenty of hay."

Erik tugged at Papa's jacket. "Are we still going to see our land today?" he asked.

"Yes," said Papa. "But first, let's unload the wagon. The horses don't need to pull any extra weight. Remember, they've had a long journey too."

Mr. Larson heard the eagerness in Erik's voice. He smiled and said, "Why not borrow our horses and wagon? I'll unhitch your team while you're gone, and we can unload the wagon later. I think Erik will feel better once he's seen the land."

They hitched up the Larsons' horses and set off. Just before they reached their land, Papa said, "Now close your eyes, and don't open them until I tell you."

Erik felt the wagon bump and rattle along a rutted path. Once or twice he was tempted to open his eyes, but he gripped the wagon seat harder and kept them shut. Finally the wagon ground to a halt.

"We're here!" said Papa proudly. In front of them was a small clearing surrounded on all sides by trees. A few stumps showed, evidence of Papa's work. In the distance, Erik could just see the lake twinkling in the sunlight.

"Oh, it's just as lovely as you described it!" exclaimed Mama. Erik grinned. He'd never seen a better piece of land in his whole life. He couldn't believe it was really all theirs!

"We still have a lot to do in the next few weeks," said Papa. "Winter can come early in Minnesota. We want to be ready for it."

"Where are we going to build our house and barn?" asked Erik. The family spent some time choosing the best places for the buildings.

"Our first home will be a log cabin," explained Papa. "It will be quick to build and good enough for the winter. Later we can work on a house like Uncle Anders has."

Papa pointed out the trees he had cut down in the summer. He explained to Erik how people would saw them into logs of the same length. Next they would cut a square off each log and carve notches on the top and bottom of each end. Then the logs would be ready to stack into a house. When the cabin was built, they would finish it by stuffing sticks, wood chips, and mud into the gaps between the logs.

"To keep the wind out?" asked Anna.

"That's right," Papa replied.

Erik turned and looked at all the land. Even though it was mostly wooded now, he imagined what it would look like in a few years. He saw fenced-in pastures filled with cows and sheep. He pictured fields where corn grew as high as a forest. He felt the joy of fishing in the lake. And he saw a real house and a barn. In his mind, he pictured his family sitting by the fireplace inside their cozy cabin during the cold Minnesota winter. Erik couldn't wait to start building that cabin. America was going to be a wonderful place to live!

Kandiyohi County, Minnesota
December 14, 1869

Dear Grandma and Grandpa,

It's our first winter in our new home. Everyone except Freya helped to build it. She's too little, but she walks now and is always getting into mischief. There's a blizzard outside, but we're snug inside.

Papa is working at the lumber camps again this winter. Don't worry, though. We have good neighbors nearby who are always ready to help. They're Swedish too.

I miss you a lot and wish you were here. Give Tip a hug when you see him.

Love,
Erik

Sweden in the 1860s

Although Erik and his family are fictional characters, this story is based on actual events. In the 1800s, the population of Sweden grew steadily. The amount of farmland did not. Then in the 1860s, the weather caused a series of crop failures. This left farmers unable to feed their families. Many families decided to try their luck in America, where there was more land. More than 60,000 Swedes made the journey to the United States between 1867 and 1869. Most settled in the Midwest.

Göteborg, Sweden Göteborg
is a port city on the river Gota. For
centuries, timber and iron ore from
central Sweden were floated down
the Gota. They were put on merchant
ships that sailed to other ports. In the
1840s, steamships began carrying
people and cargo. Since then, the
port has continued to grow. Each
year nearly three million people
pass through Göteborg port.

Journey to Castle Garden In 1868, Swedish ships did not
carry passengers to New York. To get to America, Swedes had to
buy tickets from a British ship line. These tickets included passage
on a ship from Göteborg to London and then a train ride across
England to Liverpool. In Liverpool, passengers boarded another
ship for New York City. It took about three weeks to travel from
Göteborg to Castle Garden in New York.

The Railroad In 1869, a railroad company advertised for workers to build rail lines in Minnesota. The ads promised $2 a day and the chance to buy land at low prices. Most workers who came to build the railroad were Swedish immigrants. Teams of sixty men cleared and laid a mile of track a day. In only a few years, Minnesota had thousands of miles of track.

Minnesota Timber Many Swedish immigrants were hired to work as lumberjacks. In winter, they cut down white pine trees and piled the huge logs near riverbanks. In spring, when snowmelt flooded the rivers, lumberjacks pushed the logs into the water. The logs floated downstream to sawmills. They were then cut into boards and used to build new settlements in the west or shipped east to cities.

WRITE A PERSONAL LETTER

In the story, Erik and Anna are nearly lost in a blinding blizzard. Imagine you are Erik or Anna. Write a letter to a friend in Sweden telling about your adventure.

- Copy the chart below.

- Using the information from the story, write the events in the boxes in the order they happened.

- Write your account of events using clue words such as *first, next, then,* and *last* to show the sequence of events.

- Use words that describe your feelings about what happened.

1
2
3
4
5

READ MORE ABOUT THE MIDWEST

Find and read more books about the history of the Midwest. As you read, think about these questions. They will help you understand more about this topic.

- What happened to Swedish immigrants who settled in Minnesota?

- What other groups settled in the Midwest?

- How did the railroad affect settlement of the Midwest?

- How has the Midwest changed over time?

SUGGESTED READING
Reading Expeditions
Travels Across America's Past
The Midwest: Its History and People